The Moon Belongs To Christopher Becker

By

Robbie Taylor

ISBN: **1533477639**
ISBN-13: **978-1533477637**

DEDICATION

Thanks to Dan Willcocks for typing the manuscript, and to my publisher and friend Steve Cawte, if it wasn't for him this book wouldn't exist.

To all those people who will read this book and not ask for a refund.

OTHER TITLES FROM BLUE FROG PUBLISHING

Struggling Up The Hill by Robbie Taylor

Poetry From The Pub by Lincoln Writers Collective

Hitchcocks Baby by Steve Cawte

Insert Suitable Title Here by Steve Cawte

The Wisdom of Apple Thieves by Robbie Taylor

The Age of Jack by Robbie Taylor

Blue Frog Publishing are an East Midlands-based publishers for more information contact bluefrogpublishing@gmail.com

The Moon Belongs To Christopher Becker

OTHER TITLES FROM THIS AUTHOR

Struggling Up The Hill by Robbie Taylor

Poetry From The Pub by Lincoln Writers Collective

Blue Frog Publishing are an East Midlands-based publishers for more information contact bluefrogpublishing@gmail.com

Robbie Taylor

The Moon Belongs To Christopher Becker

I want to laugh back at the world
for all it's done to me.
For all it's hurled at me. Wouldn't that be fun?
To laugh at the black cloud and the lightning bolt
because I'm too proud to admit it's really my fault.
Now that's funny. To think I have pride.
Shameless of me to think I'm blameless.
And yet I cling on to this little thing,
even though my self-respect has long since died.
It wasn't always so.
Once upon a time, the world and I had got on finely.
The world was warm and shiny. It smiled on me,
without wanting nothing in return
and how I danced beneath its indifference,
it's occasional glance.
How I understood gravity, the opportunities of chance,
serendipity and touching wood.
The world left me to find my own luck,
to take the paths I took, and we understood each

other.

I had known my place, I would never bite the hand
      that feeds, spit in its invisible face.

And then you noticed me, took an interest, meddled.

Thanks world. Give me a moment, and I will laugh
      back at you.

Because I understand the joke now. I understand it all,

and yet I understand nothing, except I have to be
      broken before you will let me fall, to land at your
      feet.

And I am falling.

It has been six or seven, maybe eight years since her
      whose name I cannot say decided to take my
      faith away.

And yet it is her who I think about every single day.

I pretend my worship is a red hot hate. But it's not,

because in our end, self-delusion is all I've got.

I'm too intelligent to believe in mind tricks and illusion,

but too thick to stop them taking charge.

I will always find sticks with which to beat myself.

I will always find bricks to throw through my own
      windows.

I will always find kicks to give to myself, I know the
   soft spots to hit, can join the dot-to-dots that
   reveal this worthless bag of shit.
And it's all because of her.
It started with her, I'm still living with her, and I will die
   with her.
I am falling, and the departed will laugh.
And on broken knees I will say the name of her whose
   name I cannot say, for those letters are the
   disease that has no cure.

I mouth my mantra that temporarily dispels her from
   my thoughts.
That fells this colossus, while I hate myself for
   succumbing to my losses, my defeats. At how
   readily I catch the bolts the world tosses, how
   steadily I stand beneath its clouds.
I hate myself for so meekly accepting my descent.
And I am tired.
Not for want of sleep, but tired of what is required to
   live a life.
I am tired of fighting the memories that we don't want
   to keep, that cut us deep with the sharpness of a

midnight knife.

I am tired of being me, with my friends and family.

These chess pieces that don't follow the rules.

These hollow, sordid queens and where the kings are
fools.

I am tired of these morbid mortals, who too easily
accept death, who crave it so they can worship it
at its altar, so they can venerate the dead.

Before the gift of a corpse, they will take back all the
bad words they ever said, they will paint a
brighter picture. Brush a glow around his head
and kneel before their newly crowned saint.

And they are looking at me now.

Berating me with their tear-filled eyes, waiting for me
to kiss the dead, to kiss my dad goodbye,

to stare into his face, and with a final kiss chase away
the myth that love conquers all.

But he cannot be woken.

They look at me.

An unspoken order for me to attend the dead, but
there are no dutiful steps towards his bed.

I am stood with my shadow against the wall, and if
they ever understood me at all, they would not
ask me to kiss the dead.

11

I knew this moment would arrive, but as I could never
  recall ever kissing my dad when he was alive,
  what was the point now?
Why should I anoint flesh as cold dead as it was when
  living, giving a final kiss because I've been told
  to, because it's expected, because the defences
  my dad had erected were finally down.
They had gladly given their pretences of love, their
  mediocre sentences, their kisses from the
  manual of the bereaved, and if they know that I
  can't be so easily deceived, then they should not
  ask me to kiss the dead.
We had never been a tactile family. Dad had never sat
  me on his knee,
he had never read aloud to me, never once said he
  was proud of me.
I found my treasure islands in the library.
I found my pleasures beyond the family tree.
So I had never bonded with my dad, he had never
  offered the opportunity.
My dad preferred his children to be rarely seen and
  barely heard,
and so between my sister and I, we hardly knew this
  man.

He never once said I love you, not even in a whisper.

Not even in response to something similar we may
have said.

So if they were familiar with me at all, they would not
ask me to kiss the dead.

My sister had erased the barren wastes of our
childhood.

She had based her life around being the good
daughter, swallowing the myths that he had
taught her.

She has learnt to relish the bitter taste of memory.

To savour the denial, to accept his behaviour was
normal,

and she adopts the formal postures seen in the pages
of happy family magazines, fixes her face with a
housewife's smile that's both cowardly and
obscene.

She loved Dad, because that was a good daughter's
duty.

But I couldn't get past the confusion and ambiguity,

for I saw through the smoke and mirrors

and knew which words would choke us both if said out
loud.

These illicit words, these unnecessary words.

So Dad and I were complicit in an unspoken oath, not
to say what wasn't really there.
So why invent reasons to say these tokens that will
not be meant?
How will a kiss now save what was always broken?
But if my family want to say these words around his
bed, that's fine.
But if they know these words were never mine, then
they should not ask me to kiss the dead.
They look at me, accusing eyes that say that I don't
care.
That I'm selfish, that I don't want to share in their
pantomime.
And how dare my sister use guilt to try and shame
me.
Saying my dad is the only dad I ever had,
but I'm not playing that game.
Not when our relationships were built on indifference.
We were the sad clowns, and Dad the stilt man in our
circus whose strides were always eating up the
distance as he tried to shirk us to stay just out of
reach.
Ignoring the persistence of a child who is imploring on
bended knees, and begging for a piece, a

morsel of acknowledgement.

For him to look down and wipe away the tears of a
sad faced clown.

I am mad at her for trying, for ignoring the fact that
these are feelings I never had.

He was never the dad I wanted him to be, not even in
the end.

You want me to be sad, and I am.

I am sad for being me.

And I was never feared by his coming death,

but I was scared of his final breath. Of what it may
contain.

Scared of an unwanted apology, to not stopping him
having the final say,

to have the final move in our endgame. To checkmate
me.

To berate me with a final breath filled with God-fearing
self-blame and remorse, pretending to God he
feels shame and regret for the actions that set
the course for the toppling of the king, reaching
out, but not to me.

It is all too late. As his family stood watching the life
leaking out from him through every pore, and
where his only son will come to hate his sister,

mum and brother-in-law for beseeching him to
come and kiss the dead.

To place his lips on cold and clammy skin, to colour in
the grey to kiss the sin away, to let the grieving
begin.

And I was scared his last breath may have me
believing in redemption.

Even though I know there can be no exemption for a
father's sin.

For his sin is not freed by death.

It is magnified by its inexistence instead, by its
smugness that retribution is now denied.

And if he knew that his last breath would blow us to
his too-big bed, then he should know better than
anyone, not to ask me to kiss the dead.

I watch my family.

I watch each of them bend down and place their lips
on my dad's cheek, his forehead.

I watch them as they speak the words I know, but
cannot hear, my mum, my sister and my
brother-in-law. A sad little procession around his
bed,

who give their last kiss and last goodbye.

A last reach. A last chance to leave an impression of

themselves,

and still I stand by the door.

Watching my brother-in-law take my mother's hand

I am trying not to laugh at this kiss and tell.

Because I know all is not well in the house of kisses
for the dead,

and I know their wishes to rest in peace and other
clichés are futile words, expected words,
selected words from poems and plays and
religious myth. These invidious, refined words of
fake prophets, designed to frighten the
enlightened, to make profit with their worthless
power, to take ownership of that final hour, for
these words are for comfort, these are words to
be noticed by the living.

And as I watch from the doorway, I look at this empty
bag of skin that used to be my dad and I realise
that I had once loved what lay within, and hope
that one day I will know exactly why.

But I will not lie now.

I will not pretend that I've lost a friend.

I will not fill the silence with words I do not feel.

I will not send him on with this deceit, this is not the
day to hand him my defeat, not here.

This is his city.

And I will not dishonour him by giving him my false
    self-pity

for I am not forgiving of either of us

and neither will I pamper to the living, my family,

these remainders,

these three who are over-awed by the death that has
    chained us to this corpse.

This remnant that refused to be ignored.

And yet despite these chains, we are divided

because I haven't decided if the pain of grieving is
    inside me, if I'm even capable,

or that I will be leaving without giving him my final
    embrace,

or if I will go face-to-face with the man who holds my
    future. The man who knows what lies for me
    ahead.

But my family will not hear my goodbyes, so they
    should not ask me to kiss the dead.

I resent their tears, because they're real.

Because they're behaving how you're meant to feel.

Would I even have any tears to come?

And as I watch my sister, brother-in-law and mum
    wipe their dutiful eyes, I realise I don't.

There will be no beautiful lies from my too-honest
    eyes.
Their eyes don't see that it's all too late.
That tears will not rehydrate this husk that lies in state,
and as I watch my sister, my brother-in-law and mum,
I think about the conversations that are bound to
    come.
Their looks of dismay that I march to the sound of my
    own drum,
that I play the music of a one-man- band.
And I recall how it had been my brother-in-law who
    had held my mother's hand.
Well fuck them if they think I'll play at happy families
    now.
Fuck them if they think they'll turn this into a family
    row.
Fuck them their righteous tears, and their wasted
    years.
Fuck them for grieving for the life they've lost.
Fuck them for not knowing what an 'I love you' cost.
Fuck them. Fuck my dad.
Look at the lives you never had, of lives undone.
Daughters, wives and son. Fuck them all.

I stand there and feel my heart miss a beat.

And in that missing beat, I know

there will be no kisses for the dead.

No genuflections at his feet.

No pretended recollections or historical reflections,

no smoothing out the imperfections because I realise I
    am done.

I am too tired to be the son.

I will not be a part of this family anymore.

My mum, my sister and my brother-in-law don't need
    me.

They have each other to carry the flame, their torch of
    lies to burn away the blame.

And I will not reach to ignite that fire, and keep it
    alight.

It is no longer my fight, so leave me be.

I will find a deserted beach where I will be stronger
    than you.

I will resist arms trying to pull me. I will surround
    myself with an ocean

because you don't need me, you have the
    presentation of emotions to keep you busy. So
    go shake the hands, go and weep, go and make

the right noises.

But most of all, remember the choices made around
     his bed.

Remember that you never heard the goodbyes said
     between a father

and his son. So please, don't ever ask me to kiss the
     dead.

I turn my back on them and walk away

even though my dad is dead, I have nothing to say.

I have a million words. But nothing to say.

As always, my mind is on her whose name I cannot
     say.

I am remembering her days.

I am remembering her leaving.

I cannot mourn my dad's passing,

until she's dead, then I will stop grieving for her.

She will always hold the key to this home-made jail.

Its bars are the restraints of her betrayal.

A condemned man can stand tall against his post

for it is betrayal, not death that we fear the most

and I am condemned, I know.

Dad's death is just another nail, another exercise for

me to fail, the more chance for lies to be told,

yet another ghost for me to hold.

I just want to go home to my bed, where these

phantoms can have free run inside my head

inside my head inside my head inside my head

inside my head inside my head inside my head

inside my head inside my head inside my head

inside my head help me inside my head inside

my head inside my head inside my head inside

my head inside my head inside my head inside

my head inside my head runs blood that burns

in black streams of red inside my head inside

my head inside my head inside my head inside

my head inside my head are the thunderous

echoing dreams of the new-born dead inside my

head inside my head inside my head inside my

head inside my head inside my head is my too

big bed where I would turn to bare shoulders

and watch you sleep knowing I can't reach you

in your floating deep, did you dream in colour,

was I the villain in black and white, twirling my

cape and moustache, in the endless fog of

endless night, I hated the doors you hid behind,

that shut me out from the worlds you make, and

while in those lawless lands, which of our
promises did you break, what comforts did you
find as I watched you sleep, because I would
turn to bare shoulders and watch you in your
floating deep, knowing that in my own I may not
find you there, because these worlds you made,
were never mine to share, inside my head inside
my head inside my head inside inside my head I
need to get home because I know ghosts who
aren't really dead.

I'm not going to work today. In fact, I'm never going
     back.
There's no point.
I have a million words and nothing to say.

I realise the last of my friends has given up on me.
Good. It is a relief. I'm tired of pretend, of living a life
     that fits in the puzzle.
I'm not on Facebook, I've stopped using my phone,
     answering the door.
I'm Greta Garbo, leave me alone.

Paint it black like a rolling stone.

I'm Greta Garbo leave me alone, I'm Old Mother
Hubbard eating her own bone, do you know
good old Greta, do you, have you met her, did
you ever get her, did you, did you, because
inside my head nothing is understood in the
streaming blood that runs black red so leave me
alone, because me and the world both knew but
never said we were meant to be friends for long.

We never built ourselves a den, we never had a
favourite song

There were no special handshakes, no honour-bound
swears.

Neither interested in the revelations, from midnight
truth or dares.

There were no oaths of Brotherhood, no palms
pressed in smears of blood,

we never sprayed our names on bridge supports, or
carved initials into wood.

There are no second chances with the world, it
doesn't hear what words you have to say.

We just drift on its carefree wind.

Until it decides to blow the summer of us away.

It gave me her whose name I cannot say, but not to
    keep, it never lets you keep unless you put its
    gifts inside your head inside your head inside
    your head.

I'm going back to bed.

As a shooting star disturbs the sky
and the world is covered in fresh snow,
I now know you were never here for me to keep,
that you were never here for me to let you go.

Her whose name I cannot say has come early today.
Zip a dee doo dah and a hip hip hooray.
I am going back to bed.
I lay here, an outstretched arm with empty haul,
a single shadow against the wall and her whose name
    I cannot say is not really here at all.

I could cope if she was dead.

I wouldn't be haunted then, by succubus and
abominations.

Taunted with my self-induced hallucinations.

Inside my head is where I give them life.

I bring forth those black magic conjurations, give
shelter to these eternal creations.

I have a terminal disease that eats the unforgiving, the
fever of the foolish who try to bury the living.

I wear my horsehair and my magician's hat, because I
have turned you into Schrödinger's cat.

Of course you're real, I'm not stupid. But you're not
real, and I am stupid and lost

inside my head. I am stupid and lost.

I step on the cracks in pavements, because the world
is too large.

In the galaxy shine of lonely midnights I howl at the
man in the moon because I dare to feel the
lightning charge and tell him to save a slice of
cheese because I'm coming soon with a book of
stories for us to read, pages turning by the world
as it blows its breeze around and beyond us and
we will watch our loved ones bleed no more.

There are no letters on the doormat.
No missed calls.
No ghosts are knocking at my door. Inside my head I
hear the whistle of wind through empty halls.
I think I'll make some toast.

Fuck off.

I saw an old friend of Dad's today.
He looked at me, in me, and I knew he saw the
tumour, sat there like a black dog in a field of
snow, saw its gripping jaw and puppy eyes, he
saw this with his jazz man's soul, saw it through
eyes that had seen the eighth wonder of the
world and the Martian night.
'Tosser', he said.

I am a free man if only I didn't have this cell.
I take it everywhere, like a tortoise with his shell.
Except I can't hibernate, I've tried. Inside my head is

too alive with that red hot love I pretend is hate.

But this is my home, I'm attached to these bricks and
shadows, the creaks and ticks, the dents of
fallen arrows.

This is my home.

A hidden world, capital letters and Circus Town pretty,

built on broken dreams and the cracks of self-pity.

A sanctuary for soft lies and sunken hope,

of sweaty regrets and the drunken grope.

Three locks, two ghosts, one dream of gold.

The echoes of bodies gifted and bodies sold.

Walls that keep the secrets of a freak show tent,

with its stains of money stolen and money well spent.

And I flick on the TV, the kettle, and every light,

these welcome guests that can stay the night,

and I'm pushing against the dark, against memories
creep

because forgiveness is too costly and forgetting too
cheap.

And I know I am a story that's already been told,

three locks, two ghosts, one dream of gold.

Yeah, home. My tortoiseshell citadel.

My unbreakable fortress where her whose name I
    cannot say has only to ring the bell, because I
    always let her in.
Betrayal, I know, is not her only sin.
Just the one that hurts the most.
It is the one that puts flesh and bones onto my living
    ghost.
Betrayal is not just found in dented silver, it is borne
    from flesh and half-truths.
And you can hate when hate is love,
treachery is to be caressed in all its tooth and claw,
it catches its own tail in its eager jaw,
and in the thirst of the desert of its remains, I unwrap
    the sleeping dogs.

I feel like the disappointment found in a romantic meal
like a Poundland special that's been left on the shelf.
I feel… I'm going back to bed. Because I feel.

I went outside today. Into my back yard.
I accidentally met my new next door neighbours.
He looked attack-dog-hard and his wife like a timid

terrier.

She was sporting a black eye I assumed he gave her,

a souvenir of the hard life.

But Circus Town women were nothing but tough, their

lies running smoothly off tongues that are rough.

Because this is where I live. In Circus Town.

For this is my town, my town, this is Circus Town.

Bricks built high to hold us down,

red brick brown brick black brick cream

Lego brick Lego brick Lego brick dream.

Build and flatten and build again,

we've washed the fields down the drain.

Chop trees chop sticks chop socky chop suey,

green belt black belt hong kong phooey.

Follow the yellow brick road to Benefit Street,

visit the benefit of the doubt and the benefit cheat.

Big men little dogs, big chips little boxes,

the urban sprawl of urban foxes.

Scavengers, savers, opportunity wasters,

squirty cheese and lager tasters.

Salt in the blood of the salt of the Earth,

salt in the wounds from the assault of birth.

Family lines are family lies,

Jeremy Kyle and family ties,

inbred incest intermission,

look at me, I'm on television.

Ringmaster, whip master, entertainer,

juggler acrobat lion tamer.

DNA tests and DIY lives,

beating fists and cheating wives.

Punchbag punch out, punch up drunk,

smack crack brown, green and skunk,

pop pills, pop pills, pop ecstatic sweeties,

fat face, fat arse, diabetes.

Ringmaster, ringmaster whip crack whip,

faster double portions, faster double dip,

deep vein, deep fried, deep pan sizzlers,

gobble gobble gobble, turkey twizzlers.

One potato, two potato, three potato, four.

Pit stop at the chip shop and ask for more.

Cook a fresh batch in my remains

cause I've got circus town in my veins.

Eat now, die later, buy now, pay later,

nuclear family impersonator.

Tick tock tick tock Bailif's knock,

broken Britain behind broken lock,

broken lives and broken bones,

brand new trainers brand new phones.

Teenage pregnancy, teenage kicks,
knitted booties needle pricks.
One gram, two gram, three gram, four,
rock the cradle lock the door.
Midwife, good life, bad life, thug,
classless, class clown, class A drug.
Skivers divers, lodgers, dodgers,
union jacks and jolly rogers.
Fly the flag and launch the ship,
tie the bag and staunch the drip.
Learn the ropes and the three R's,
apprenticeships in stealing cars,
stolen moments, stolen pleasures,
hold on tight to golden treasures.
Red brick, brown brick, black brick cream,
dying to get out and living the dream.
The Price is Right, so come on down
for this is my town, my town. This is Circus Town.

The neighbour and his wife have gone inside.
The Wolf Man and Frankenstein's Bride.
That's how I see them, monsters manufactured,
from Hollywood and not from dreams.

Delivering the fractured screams of celluloid
but they are very real monsters, not easy to avoid.
They played friendly which is not a good thing,
not a good thing at all.
I have a funny feeling they will not stay behind their
    garden wall.
Not a good thing at all.
I'm going back to bed.

        Upon my door there comes a knock
            a visitor awaits
        Upon my door there comes a knock
          a visitor that's never late
        Upon my door there comes a knock
           I sit and do not rise
        Upon my door there comes a knock
           I sit with open eyes
        Upon my door there comes a knock
           my visitor needs no key
        Upon my door there comes a knock
          my visitor has come for me
        Upon my door there comes a knock
          I don't hear the tread of feet
        Upon my door there comes a knock
          I don't get up to greet

Upon my door there comes a knock
my visitor has no goodbyes
Upon my door there comes a knock
My visitor is here, and closes both my eyes.

I wake up with a girlish squeal.
Inside my head, her whose name I cannot say, is
laughing at me.

I haven't thought of her once today – shit.

Leave me be.

Leave me be.

Leave me.

Circus Town is crying. Not for me.

It is crying because that's what mother's do

for children denying to heed the word of their
protector.

The scattered seed that turns it's back,

the battered eggshells of the defector.

For I am living in the land of the broken dreams of
others,

of absent father's and disappointing mothers.

I'm living in the land of the scream and the shout,

of the upside down and the inside out.

I'm living in the land of the non-returnable and the
dispossessed,

of the home sweet home of the repossessed.

I'm living in the land of the outstretched hand and the
collecting tin,

of the shining time and the instant win.

I'm living in the land of new myths and old wive's
tales,

of washed away people and washed up whales.

I'm living in the land of artificial life and videoed death,

of children who squander their father's last breath.

I'm living in the land of the contender and the
wannabe,

of the gold leaf IOUs plucked off the money tree.

I'm living in the land of the expired lease of the one
     more chance,
of the fading music of the night's last dance.
I'm living in the land of the Bailiff's knock and
     squatters rights.
For those of you who decide to stay
would you please turn off the lights?

But where would I go? Where would I go?
Because Circus Town is all I know.
It's all I need, and I can survive
if I keep my head low.

I am a citizen of Circus Town
I have a rich man's cravings,
on a poor man's savings, I like that. I ought to write it
     down
before I got back to bed.

I thought faces were supposed to fade in time,
become nebulous in the clouds of your mind,

well hers hasn't. No, not hers.

Her whose name I cannot say has a vivid face.

A vivid, vivid face.

I see it in clouds, and bark, and mayonnaise,

and inside my head inside my head inside my head

she comes as a livid scar of unwithered red,

so I chant my mantra to remove the itch.

That wondrous thunderous plunderous bitch.

She thieves into me so I will feel her,

the stealer the squeaker the double dealer

and I loved you like a poet once,

I sailed over emerald oceans, on the air of just a sigh.

I laid you down in gentle folds, on the clouds that
floated by.

I was lifted on your cadence, on a brush of whispered
heat,

I stormed Olympus, and laid slain gods before your
feet.

And when the day had run its course, putting down its
head,

you would keep alight the darkness, with promises
unsaid .

And I would listen to the silence, the quiet of a waiting
kiss,

before I would dream of a world, where this is all there
is,
because this is how I loved you once, with a poet's
love.
A romantic's love that captured gods above.
I was a fool for a skipping heart, for the heat of a
fevered brow,
for this is how I loved you once, you stupid fucking
cow.
She has a vivid face
A vivid face.
Mantra mantra, chant chant, mantra.
Begone foul beast. Begone. Begone. begone
Take your midnight feast and morning song.
Take back all the lies you ever said,
and your vivid face that's inside my head inside my
head inside my head inside my head.

The neighbour.
The neighbour came around today
but I left his knock ignored.
Whatever he wants I know it's something I can't
afford.

And who does he think he is anyway?
Who does he think I am?
Who does he think really shot Kennedy?
Too whit too who too whit to who I'm the secret
      gunman and the twit is you.
So go away Mr Wolf man, go away. Shoo.
Go and blow down someone else's door,
because Circus Town is crying once more,
cause that's what mother's do.
It's crying Mr Wolf Man and this time it's for me.
Circus Town is crying me a river of blood
because,

I know the concept of friendship
but I am bereft of the manual and so I am left
with acquaintances and a brother

He is not my friend, we are thick with blood
only together in the places we once stood
in photographs, taken by our mother

I have a father, but he is not my friend
he never bent his back, allowing me to ascend
onto shoulders, I thought could hold the world

We had never baited hooks or flew a kite
I never waited up for a kiss goodnight
and never held a hand, hidden beneath fingers tightly
curled

They fuck you up, your mum and dad is a famous line
that I've always refused to adopt as mine
until memories decide to call

but blame can come too easily
and is relatively free, it is ripe fruit
plucked from the family tree, before it has time to fall

and childhood friends are just friends of chance
and like the prettier memories of a first romance
they were never meant to last

There are billions of stars in all my skies
but they're not my friends for when I close my eyes,
their existence ends, for I have left them to their past

You could be my friend, I could try to be yours
and I would add harmonies to the scores,

that drive a one man band

If we would be friends, we could watch the wheels
turn
leading to a place where I may learn
how unfurled fingers make a hand

There are a billion stars in all my skies
but I only need one to fall before my eyes
to let me shine against the black

and if we had a child, you and I
would it be my friend? I do not know,
but before that child reaches childhood's end
I would have learnt to bend my back

Can you hear me laughing Mr Wolf Man, you sucker?
Can you hear me laughing you gullible fucker?
I have no brother I have no brother I have no dad.
She is gone and my dad is dead my dad is dead,
and you're knocking on the door that's inside my head
inside my head inside my head inside my head
and Circus Town's tears are those of laughter
at me or with me I just don't care, because I'm falling

into the past because there is no after, there is no
    next
there is just her and him and words too easily unsaid.

I'm going to bed.

I thought I was coping with not coping.
Oh I know there's the self-indulgent whingeing and
    whining.
The pining for the living, but overall…
I thought I was a fully paid-up member of the falling
    club,
bought the club tie and paid all my fees,
but I have finally been brought to my knees…
by a light bulb.
And my panic isn't because my bathroom is dark,
I'm acting totally manic, screaming in frustration, I rant
    and shout for the simple reason I've got to go
    out.
I don't want to venture into Circus Town,
so I turn the house upside-down.
I bang and tear open cupboard doors, hunt through
    shelves and cluttered drawers,
I found eighty six pence and a celebrity magazine I'd

never seen before.

God knows how it ended up in my bottom drawer, I
    hate them with a passion.

What do I want with nonentities and unaffordable
    blackmail fashion?

I flick through it to confirm what I've always known.

not in the bathroom obviously,

because the fucking bulb had blown,

and who pays the price for the wages of sin,

that are found in the pages within,

where the stories and tales of their glories and fails

is the toss in the gloss of a celebrity magazine.

Here we find the one-track-mind of the one-trick-pony,

the before and after of the once-too-fat and the now-
    too-bony, who smiles with canned laughter at
    the flunky and the crony, and at the performing
    monkey leading the entourage, who will sell her
    out in the blink of an eye, because that's what
    happens when you put a junkie in charge.

And on this page we find the thousand yard stare

as she has trouble getting drunkenly out the back of a
    car

with the inevitable flash of the stubble rash of her
    pubic hair, as her G-string is disappearing down

her ass,

one accompanied by an overbearing clown who thinks

he's upper class, who's strung out on designer

smack, this class-A couple of the magazine

rack.

Page after page of too slim bodies and dim nobodies,

the underfed and the underage whose every whim for

exposure is given a stage.

We have the pictures of the bad hair day,

the glad we're gay and have finally come out because

they've exhausted all the stories of speculation

and doubt, and people know they're hiding

behind the closet door,

and the pictures of those who deny they preferred the

way they looked before

the hiring of the IT geek for touching up or butching up

a wayward cheek, then firing the PA for daring

to speak about the photoshopped frogs

for this is the world of the sadly betrayed and the

madly portrayed, with their happy yappy dogs.

Another turn of the page and another black magic

face for us to point at and laugh.

Here's the so -called tragic case of a super model

giraffe who has fled the zoo and is now a basket

case, from beach shoots to bleached out roots
and seen shoving a McDonald's down her face.
Page after page of the nipple slip, the unwaxed lip, the
uncoordinated colours of an acid trip, the pop
star shits who have no hits, displaying tattoos
and their girlfriend's new tits, trying to score free
booze as they gate-crash the Brits.
We see a himbo vs a bimbo in the shortest ever battle
of wits, but the desperate and ruthless aren't
necessarily clueless and so only have
themselves to blame, and they can never be
lonely when they're searching for fame, and they
only mutiny when they don't get the scrutiny
they seek because they know the name of the
business is show.
I see all the lies and the cellulite thighs and with my
own bombarded eyes I see the unmasked,
unhealthy, unguarded lives of people I really
don't want to know
and I sigh in exasperation at all this desperation and
dismay at how we've become a nation who will
pay for this shit and drivel for one golden
English pound.
So is it our stupidity that is feeding their cupidity with

our need for pictures of accidental nudity that
keeps the wheels of celebrity spinning round.
Because we bay for our fix for salacious pics of the
wink and the blink from girls seeking exposure
by forgetting their knix, because they know all
about openings and nothing about closure,
and we demand to see the undoing of seams and the
second-hand dreams of those has beens and
WAGs, the scream queens and hags with their
party scene bags, the hale and the hearty, the
pale Glitterati and the prince at the party
dressed up as a nazi, and the glimpse of the
money maker by the upskirt paparrazi
all so we can get our kicks
up skirt, downshirt, prettify and testify and dish the
dirt.
This is what we want from the magazines we take
down off the shelves,
but would we be so impressed if the secrets
confessed, and the pictures of the unwary and
partially undressed, we're the result of turning
the cameras on ourselves.

The magazine has put me in a dark place

and I don't mean the bathroom.
On the bright side, I feel I can face Circus Town.

I was wrong
I hate every fuckin' body
I'm going to bed

I

AM

GOING TO

BED

I wake up with a jolt
Her whose name I cannot say strode through my
     dreams, she was twelve foot tall and belching
     my name like an alpha toad.
I chant the mantra to keep her quiet, to shoo her away
     before I can listen to what she has to say.
She has brought her own soundtrack.

I don't recognise the song but I dance to its tune
and fix a smile on my face like the man in the moon.

I'm as tall as my name, but shrink when I hear her say
        it out loud
and I try not to struggle in case I wrinkle my shroud.
My friends are no friends, are your friends not mine,
my dreams are no dreams, are your dreams to find?
My words are no words are your words to say
my sins are no sins, are your sins to pay?
My life is no life is your life to live?
How slowly I forget how easily I can't forgive.

You think you're clever, that I'm your puppet on a
        string,
I chant my mantra I chant my mantra and hear you
        sing along
I chant it louder,
inside my head I chant it louder.

In the dark corners in the black alleys of my mind
you lurk

you wait in the shadows of the once upon a time,
you squat

amongst the rubble of missing days and faceless
      names,
you stalk
in the half-sung lines of childhood games,
you live.
I cannot kill you inside my head inside my head.
I cannot kill you.

Shit.

I spoke to the neighbours today.
I had a million words and yet had nothing to say.
He did. He jabbered and blabbered with his scalpel
      voice
it was all the crackle and static of white noise, but
      some words got through.
The Wolf Man has a human name,
Frankenstein's Bride has got one too.

I can't remember them now.

And somehow I gave him mine.

I'm not impolite, I just hate the world and every fucker
      in it,

but I'm not impolite.

His wife stood beside him like a broken sparrow,

nose too thin and eyes too narrow,

she was too busy with tics and twitches.

I've never done drugs in my life, not for moral
      reasons, more for financial ones,

but I'm pretty sure the new neighbour and his wife had
      fully embraced this aspect of Circus Town life,

but some words got through some words got through

little puzzles little puzzles without a clue,

they are guttural bricks and sibilant sighs

and I try to circumnavigate the truths and lies,

but in unsyncopated rhythms these faithless words

take flight with the ungainly wings of startled birds,

they perch on the precipice above my falling ground,

the sparrow and the wolf sharpening claws into
      sculpted sound,

and despite all my attempts they pierce and rest
      inside me

because I don't know a mantra to chant that would

hide me,
they are gone but they're still here
more ghosts inside my head inside my head.
I sit in my chair and look at the joint the Wolf Man has
given me.

It's nearly tea time and I haven't thought about her
whose name I cannot say once.
Shit – I can't believe I fell for that one again.

I am at the doctors tomorrow.
I won't let him touch me, he doesn't need to touch me.
Not to prescribe my medication. My happy pills,
fuck me is that ironic.
I'm not depressed I told him last time.
I'm just moronic, just not blessed with the ability to
ignore the futility, the ugliness that is created by
spilled seed.
'Oh Mr Becker' he had said, 'you're very depressed
indeed.'
But he doesn't have to touch me.
I can tell him that it hurts to love, that it hurts more not

to try,
it hurts to live, hurts more not to die,
it hurts to push, to pull, to enter the fight,
it hurts to rush to dull the sharp edge of night,
it hurts to breathe in, it hurts to breathe out,
it hurts to be heard over a silent shout,
it hurts to love, it hurts more not to die,
he doesn't need to touch me to know that.
I finally put the bulb in the bathroom.
I think I preferred the mammalian gloom.
It's too white.
She was naked in this room.
Shut up stupid shut up shut up shut up and chant the
        mantra and shut up and chant the mantra,
I will go and see
I will go and see if the wolf
I will go and see If the Wolf man
I will go and see if the Wolf Man is home.

He passes me the joint .
I can hear a voice. It's mine. It's going yakkety yakkety
        yakkety yack. I'm Thomas the Tank Engine a
        chug chug chugging down the track and over
        the bridge and coming back belching smoke out

my smoking stack and I go choo choo choo and
a clackety clack and I go a choo choo choo and
a clackety clack
but how I had promised, and promised and promised
not to talk about myself,
but Mr Wolf Man with his own lighter and baccy pouch
has given me his wares and buy now pay later
couch, and because never is a promise that's'
just someone else's last wish, so I go a yakkety
yakkety to Circus Town's latest therapist.
But I had promised not to talk about myself, that I
would never bare my soul, to spray my words
like an aerosol, it's mist landing on more saintly
heads without you understanding that these
words so faintly said are my loud and screaming
devils demanding to be heard from inside my
head inside my head inside my brain with the
decibel levels of a steaming belching relentless
train that runs on the bile of her name and the
denial of blame, on unwanted anger and
unwarranted hate.
There are no stops on this line, I can't afford
passengers to board a train where I'm the only
destination,

and I had promised but the Wolf Man walks the walk
of Circus Town.
But I had promised and you can trust me.

But I have oiled these rusty tracks, that were built to
carry my freight, my panic attacks. My lonely
hate, my manic depression, my first impression
and the last confession.
This train carries my weight and yet here we are. I've
lied.
I look at the Wolf Man with a wicked thought.
'You can't get off this ride because your ticket's
bought and you've taken the seat. You can't get
off till I do Mr Wolfman – coo coo ca fucking
choo'.
I want to shake my fist in silent protest at Circus
Town, but the Wolf Man is a toxicological
therapist who has induced the millions of words
that have nothing to say, these token words that
nest in my brain like broken birds, and if they
could speak from their grasping beaks they
would tell you that I'm not quite right, I'm brittle,
a little bit off, that I'm sick but not insane, I don't

sit and lick the window pane, the rain slicked
glass on this accelerating train, I just sit with her
whose name I cannot say waiting for the weight
to pass.
So why talk now?
Why talk now when I said there would be no
disembarkation from inside my head inside my
head, pulling up at the Circus Town station?
There has been no one pestering me to reveal the
festering boiling hate I feel in every bone, soiling
myself with the shit which is all I've ever known.
But should I deprive you?
Should I deprive you entry to these dark places alive
with the stark faces of those I've loved and
betrayed?
Should I tell you of the dirt of my despair, the lack of
care, the smack of hands both free and bare,
and dare you to understand these stories and
not to take for granted the pointless stakes I've
planted in this wonderland of a pointless life and
pointless glories?
Should I tell you this Mr Wolf Man, Mr Therapist?

Should I tell you about the thoughts that are no longer
mine?
How I'm always a little out of sorts, how I've crossed a
line, been tossed into the arms of mental
derangement that does not have the charms of
a gentle arrangement because I scream and rail
I scream and rail because in my dreams I fail to
catch the comet's tail of hope that is always just
out of reach as it's screeching through my black
skies before it vomits and dies, flickering out its
spew of friendless light, finally spluttering out on
the sands of my desert island beach of endless
night.
But I had promised.
I had promised not to play this game.
Not to speak the millions of words with nothing to say,
so everything is running fine on the Circus Town line,
where death is truth and life is lies
otherwise I would give you the list of names of those
I've betrayed, enticed into games I've played,
and played not too nice, the loaded dice, the ace
up the sleeve, all with a face you couldn't
possible believe could deceive, I've portrayed
the sinner the boozer the winner and the loser,

I've rubbed dirt into the cricket ball and because
it's my show, I've had a front row seat to it all.
These defeats have always been mine, and that's fine
that's fine because the front row seats are
reserved for liars and cheats, and I've deserved
my place
we all have history Mr Wolf Man

and I had promised mine would remain a mystery. I
would keep it to myself ,
I don't want to be another misery memoir on the shelf,
a grimoire of propaganda and unwanted
candour and bleating heart that's about as
welcome as a Christmas fart,
and yet here I am,
and yet here I am playing the favourite game of
parental blame, but that's okay that's okay coo
coo ca fucking choo because I'm a little bit
mental Mr Wolf Man and history is all the same.
It is the cheating wife the heart heart heart
heartbeating life with its pulse pulse pulse of the
repeating defeating doubt that follows me
swallows me and that's beat beat beating in the
hollow of me,

and I know I'd rather not share the lies I have,
      because they are the only truths I've got.
We all have a story to tell, to manipulate and sell.
We are born and we die, it's only the middle that's the
      lie, it is bent and moulded, we fiddle until the
      truth is spent and folded into something we can
      present to the world.
But I had promised not to talk. I did. I did. I did.
It is my choice not to sing to the baby birds in my brain
      the millions of words that have nothing to say,
I have made her whose name I cannot say a diva, a
      star, this unwithered red wound of an
      unblistered scar,
but I am giving it all Mr Wolf Man, coo coo ca fucking
      choo.
I am giving you more than the gist, I'm giving an
      unexpurgated list of the malignant tumours that
      haunt me with indignant humours and I am
      weighted down by pros and cons of the unsung
      songs I promised I would never sing, with their
      lyrics of a past built on sex and lies and the half-
      hearted attempts to exorcise these shadows that
      I cast.
So can life be good Mr Wolf Man? Can life be a

banquet and not such a crappy deal?

Or will I forever be the fuckwit with the happy meal?

I don't want to be the suck it and see guy, I want the
feasts we know sustain us, I don't want to suckle
on the teats of the black beasts inside my head
inside my head, because I don't want to choke
on the fast food stolen in moments, I want to
laugh back at the world, to understand the joke,
to pull up my chair and enjoy the meal. I want to
chew chew ca fucking chew Mr Wolf Man, coo
coo ca fuckin choo, and that's okay isn't it? Isn't
that okay?

The lies we fold.

I'm going to bed.

She shakes me from my sleep.

Her whose name I cannot say came in running.

She was confused.

I was on the Wolf Man's settee.

I am once more in the Wolf Man's lair.

To my dismay, there are others there.

What is this, some sort of fucking club?

A drop-in centre for circus town VIPs?

I wish they'd stayed in their sticky, thin-carpeted pub
with its two-for-ones and frozen grub, selling
illusion by the glass and Circus Town
medication which puts you top of the class in
your addiction education, instead of coming to
the Wolf Man for private tuition and the path to
graduation.

It smells of stale beer, the stink of the weak in the
Wolf Man's lair.

A girl is staring at me. She has a pink streak in her
hair and metal in her face,

it is an indifferent stare, like an undertaker closing
another coffin lid,

she has weighed me and found my balance short.

I hate her.

I want to shake her, I want her gone.

She has charity bands down both arms, she has
causes.

She invades your morality like a platoon of special
forces, for metal face is a professional protester,
a fucking volunteer for fucks sake, with a fist
always ready to shake,

I hate her because she has forgotten what she really
    believes because she believes in protest,
I hate her for the stolen ideals. For wearing air wares
    instead of heels, for that 'look at me' hair that's
    streaked with pink, but most of all, that she has
    forgotten how to think for herself, for having
    unread, unopened books on her shelf, and how
    she can't remember what she's marching for
    because another confrontation is just another
    score.
I hate her I hate her coo coo ca fucking choo
Yeah you. I hate that your 'sat on the Wolf Man's
    settee', how dare you fucking judge me you
    wannabe, how dare you look at me?
I hate you for making a heart sign with both your
    hands, showing off arms that are striped with
    charity bands, a colour chart of what you want
    us to believe, because you're wearing your heart
    on your sleeve which is always rolled up so your
    conscience is displayed and your stories told.
Everything is fair game and your coffee's fair trade
    which fuels your fire as you pray for peace in the
    world, for common sense and calm, but not
    while you've still got space on your arm. You

forcefully protest that protesting peacefully is
everyone's right, and shout that it's the police
who turn up ready for a fight as they never
forget old scores that need to be settled and
pick out their targets when everyone has been
herded and kettled, and if it's you that's been
bagged you grit your teeth getting ready to bleed
beneath the hit of a baton before being dragged
away to do the full monty where they don't even
let you keep your hat on and after you've been
stripped bare without the pretence of an arrest
you've gripped the back of a chair as a
government guest trying hard to stay clenched
because when push comes to shove it's the
fascists with their fist in the rubber gloves as
they search for megaphones and plump white
doves so put another charity band on your wrist
and unclench the cheeks of a pacifist.

You light a candle and you don't eat meat, you hug a
vandal and though you've turned your feet from
the Jesus sandal you pray for the drug user the
boozer and the child abuser because they are
people too, and because they're as special as
all of God's creations they deserve to live their

lives and so you organise your demonstrations
for those the rest of us despise as all
discrimination is criminal whether it's animal
vegetable or even mineral and so you march to
save the dolphin even though you are happy to
eat the tuna and will take it to your grave the
regret that you couldn't get to the dodo sooner
because if you're not egalitarian or vegetarian
then you're just a barbarian so put another
charity band on your wrist and shake the hand
of an activist.

You have the odd friendship band but they're not from
real friends because when a campaign is over
those friendships end and pretty stripes are all
that remain even though you've done the
sponsored walk and unsponsored run and
starved together on a hunger strike and ridden
naked through London on your bike and got in
on the hidden agendas crystallised on festival
benders that kept you energised as you stormed
the walls of the money lenders because even
though you don't have the answers you know
things need to be reformed so put another
charity band on your wrist and wave goodbye to

the optimist.

You've protested about Google after looking them up
on the internet and got arrested for believing you
could free Tibet and you want to save the
rainforests the oceans and the polar bear
because strong emotions are still not enough to
stop the world burning up like a solar flare or
prevent the possibility of an ice age returning
and you hope people are finally learning the eco
warriors are actually nice chaps and are only
cutting the fuel lines to save the ice caps and so
you just stand up jump up or lay down and hold
your ground as you're shaking your fist at the
yellow bulldozer and photobombing a selfie
taken by a fellow poser where every pacifist is
attacking hard because you'll not allow fracking
in your backyard as you call for reinforcements
on your mobile phones even though you
attacked a transmitter mast last week for
causing the cancer that might be eating your
bones so put another charity band on your wrist
because there's plenty more to go on your shit
list,

and when you see the homeless on the street you

give them a bit of change as you've always
preferred your begs to be free range and so you
stop to talk to the Big Issue seller as you know
his life but not his name and as you pass over
your coin you tell him the reasons why he's here
and who's to blame because it's the unheeded
lessons from history that mean he's now fucked
as the past is too easily forgotten and too often
overlooked and so that's why you're still banging
on about Gibralta and bloody Sunday and will be
hanging out your banners on the next Guinness
fun day as the country puts too much store on
the over-starched boys from Eton and Harrow
instead of listening more to the marching men of
Jarrow so put another charity band on your wrist
because you don't give a two bob bit for the
economist.

And you've thrown your rocks at the man in the pin-
striped suit whose stocks are his market and is
the target for your over-ripe fruit and you've
drawn a skull and crossbones on the companies
that pollute while they sponsor symphonies and
the weekend shoot and you throw your stones
grunting with the strain because fox hunting has

reared its ugly head again and it should be you
who decides what lives and dies in the
countryside where among the neat rows of
tweed wafts the protestors refrain and the sweet
nose of weed as you stand with the brother and
sisterhood waiting to ambush the gentry like a
modern day Robin Hood because it's all for one
and one for all when you're a merry man and a
musketeer because there's nothing to fear when
you know you'll never walk alone when you all
have the same protest song on your phone so
put another charity band on your wrist and see
what's left on your bucket list.

You didn't want us to go to Kuwait, Iraq, Afghanistan
but how do you think your oil gets into your
camper van because drilling and killing walk
hand in hand and it's not peace driving tanks in
the holy land and so when you write about these
places on your blog you have one foot in the
mosque and one in the synagogue and yet
refuse to accept it's religion that's wagging the
dog as you're typing in your rhubarb and custard
monologue which is just an opinion you beg
borrow or steal from other bloggers that you

follow and after you log off from these beating
chests you know there will be more dead for you
to protest about tomorrow so put another charity
band on your wrist and kick sand in the face of
the analyst.

And the worst thing is you're right. There are
questions that need to be asked, but it's hard to
hear them from behind a mask.

But we can all hear your bleeding heart a-thumping
and a-pumping as you're storming walls and
barrier jumping but is it so necessary to be
throwing your weight around when there are
better ways to make a sound and hold your
ground because when hot air is blowin' in the
wind it can just as easily set you homeward
bound and any trap can be set if you use this
right cheese and you can sign a petition to save
the trees or to show your disgust at tuition fees
and if you do manage to bring a government to
its knees make sure you remember that all dogs
have fleas so put another charity band on your
wrist because I think by now we've got the gist.

Hey, metal face, my wrists are bare.

Does that mean that I don't care?

Does that mean I'm not aware?

Or that I simply can't find a thing to wear?

Or does it mean I prefer to keep my conscience out of
sight?

That I keep my hands unheartshaped and my
footsteps light?

And do you not think you're spreading yourself too
thin, that you're heading into battles when you
don't even care if you win?

Circus Town people have always been deaf to the
rattles of a collecting tin.

And though part of me reluctantly admires the fire and
the passion within, I have to wonder which of
those charity bands represents you because
you're a fashion victim.

And I hate her I hate her I hate her I hate her I hate
her.

I hate her because underneath the pink streaks and
the metal in her face, she looks like her whose
name I cannot say.

I don't stay.

I have a million words and nothing to say.

The Wolf Man sees me to the door,
the bride of Frankenstein behind him.
She's twitching like an oscillating full stop.
He shuts me out with his human paw,
retreating into the too-full lair.
At home I sit in the throne of the deposed.
It's not. It's just a chair.
I am holding the royal sceptre of a beleaguered king.
I'm not. I am holding the see-through bag the Wolf
    Man gave me, sold me, it's all the same, it's all
    the same inside my head.
It's all the same

I am going to bed

Coo coo ca fuckin choo.
Where the hell are you Scooby Doo?
I'm a banana called Timbuctu.
I'm a coming down the track I'm a coming for you.
I'm the man in the moon and the moon is blue.
I saw the gingerbread man and said 'I love you'.
And inside my head she said 'I love you too',
Inside my head.

She said 'I love you too'.

In the morning light I breathe.

It is all that is expected,

I didn't invent the concept,

I am an end user. A consumer of someone else's

      brightness,

in the morning light there comes the dark.

Another day.

Another journey into the Wolf Man's lair.

There are other people there. New ones.

Frankenstein's Bride twitches from the kitchen door.

A new bruise smiles at me, courtesy of the Wolf Man's

      paw.

I sit opposite the three VIPs.

They are sat in a line on the Wolf Man's settee,

three wise men, three wise monkeys,

an unwritten trilogy of three Circus Town junkies.

Here they sit, staring at me, but not seeing me.

They are Scooby Doo and they've got work to do.

I decide to stay, even though I've a million words, I

      have nothing to say to the astronauts of

      Wimbledon common.

I listen…

I need another line I need another line
The drugs are fine the drugs are fine
The drugs are fine the drugs are mine
Eyes down eyes down for the old five nine
Save me a seat on the Brighton line
Come on John come on John chop me a line
Chop me a line of the mighty fine
What's that John, what's that what's that?
Is it a dog John? Is it, is it, is it a dog
Look Dave look Dave, John's got a dog
A dog Dave, a dog Dave,
What sort is it John? what sort, what sort is it?
It's a what John? a what? a fifty seven?
A fifty seven? a Heinz fifty seven?
What do you mean John? what do you mean?
Is it half spaghetti hoop and half baked bean?
Dog dog dog dog that's all you go on about
Chop me a line chop me a line
Won't you treat a brother fine?
Won't you hold me mother mine?
A dog Dave a dog Dave who has a dog Dave?
I'll tell you who Dave, Big Issue sellers have dogs
and ladies who lunch who munch and brunch

and WAGs who keep them in bags, and hags and
slags
With their brand new noses in the air
Paid for by a Russian billionaire
and they have cubic zirconia in their pubic hair
coz they think there's nothing finer
than a pimped out vagina
So chop me a line chop me a line
Chop me a line of the mighty fine
Does it bite John? Does it John? Does it bite?
Make it bite Dave John, make it bite Dave
dog dog bloody dog
Stop going on about that bloody dog
Chop me a line chop me a line
I need another line I need another line
The drugs are fine the drugs are fine
Do you kick it John? Do you? Do you kick it?
When it's bad John, do you kick it when it's bad?
Kick the dog the dog the dog the habit
The habit the habit the kick the rabbit
The rabbit the rabbit the rabbit with the habit
The rabbit does drugs the rabbit does drugs
Sliding down the fireman's pole
Hiding in his rabbit hole

Bugs does drugs bugs bugs bugs
bugs does drugs, look at his eyes Dave
His eyes Dave, look at the rabbit's eyes Dave
What does it eat John? the dog John,
What does it eat John?
Do you feed it Pedigree chum?
Do you stick things up its bum?
Do you turn it over and tickle its tum?
Do you turn it over and tickle its tum?
Do you John? Do you? Do you John?
Dog dog dog John, it's all you talk about
It looks like a Womble John, a Womble Dave
A Womble of Wimbledon common, picking up our shit
A Womble of Wimbledon common looking for a hit
So chop me a line chop me a line
Sort me out the mighty fine
Send me over the finishing line
Hit me a line hit me hit me hit me a line
Hit me hit me hit me baby one more time
Hit play hit play and play me and play me
'And play that funky music white boy'
Coz I got the moves the crazy grooves and drop the
moves
I'm more pop than Coca Cola

I'm an Elvis rock n roller

So chop me a line chop me a line

The drugs are fine the drugs are fine

The drugs are fine the drugs are mine

What's it called John? The dog John? What's it
called?

George, John? George? The dog's called George
Dave

George the dog George the Womble the Womble

The dragon the dragon the George and the dragon

the George George the Georgie Georgie

The Georgie the Porgy the Porgy the Porky

The Porky the Perky the Pinky the Pinky and the
Perky

The Perky the Twerky the Jerky the Worky

The I no Worky the I no Worky for the man

The man the suit man the fruit man

The Oh so fuckin cute man

The fair man the chair man

The chairman of the board man, the gas board

The gas man the glass man the grass man

Don't walk on the glass man

Don't break the grass man

Don't take it up the ass man

Don't turn over and take it in the ass man
Don't turn me over turn me over
I'm the astronaut man I'm the astronaut man
I'm Buzz Aldrin on his supernova
I'm buzz buzz Aldrin buzz buzz buzzing
So chop me a line chop me a line
I need another line I need another line
The drugs are fine the drugs are fine
I need to shine like sparkling wine
Credit card me a line of the old five nine
Coz I get it hard for the Brighton line
The drugs are fine the drugs are fine
The drugs are fine the drugs are mine

Fuck me John, that dog bites

Idiots

I
Am
Going to

B

E

D

A bloke came round today and bought my car.

It was arranged.

It's not like some random bloke just popped round on
      the off-chance,

if he was concerned that we did the deal through the
      letterbox, he never let on.

After all… this is Circus Town.

Her whose name I cannot say came last night.

I told her to fuck off.

Coo coo ca choo and a Scooby Doo.

Eeny meeny miney mo.

Like I have a choice.

What we can't see hurts us the most,

and yet we desire it.

She came on the chariot that pulls the sun
in flames and cloth of gold,
she said my name in spits of acid,
I held the scald of her, and felt the ice.
I spoke her name into the ash.
'Phoenix', I cried.

The Wolf Man wants me to go on a field trip.
Who does he think I am? Bear-fucking-Grylls?
But I am in the Wolf Man's grip, I have to pay my bills.
So myself, the Wolf Man, and Frankenstein's Bride,
marched forth through Circus Town looking for
where the midnight crawlers hide for we were
trawlers of men who knew the beat of the tide
and hooked the right bait.
I followed my leader feeling the weight inside,
constantly searching for the ghosts who have
not yet died, for her whose name I cannot say
would be lurking somewhere to reveal herself

and carry me away in her indifference, for I am
exposed in the Circus Town's heart, in its
workings. I want to go to bed but apparently we
have found our fellows true.

Fat Frank, Cheddar and Texas Sue, are sat on their
usual bench in the heart of Circus Town.

You would have seen them many times, even though
you walk around them with your head looking
down, because you can't catch their eyes when
you're staring at the ground.

You walk fast, a blur of shopping bags and straining
leggings hurrying past in case Circus Town's
finest are begging.

But Fat Frank, Cheddar and Tesco Sue are just sat
watching the world and its dog as it passes by

A front row seat to the suddenly shy and the busy feet
of the huddled masses who can't spare a grunt
or a nod because they've forgotten how to share
or what it's like living close to the bone and don't
know how to interact unless they have the right
app on their phone.

And some assume these bench dwellers have opted
out of humanity, that they're unemployed Big
Issue sellers destroyed by insanity. But how do

you know?

What makes you an expert when you do nothing but
quicken your strides to avoid them, before the
sour taste in your mouth can thicken your
insides so you may stomach them?

If you're one of those people who throw them the odd
coin to make yourselves feel better about your
own shitty life, fine, they'll take your coin but
have no use for your self-pity.

And though you can't help looking with guilty
superiority they know making you feel better
about yourself is not their priority.

They are taking your change, not taking on your lives,
and though you might find this strange they
have no use for those lives, the mortgages, the
gas bills, the downtrodden wives in loveless
marriages, the husbands in therapy for his
forbidden vices and the hidden expenditures of
a mid-life crisis because they've been there,
they've done all that, they've bought the t-shirt
and worn the hat, or managed to avoid it
altogether getting out before ever getting in,
getting out before forever and ever.

Fat Frank takes a can from the bag between his feet,

his face is lined and has a slight sheen of the
street.

Fat Frank is not fat at all, he's thin as a whip and six
foot three.

He'd been given his name ironically.

But he's okay with this, most nicknames are given by
people just taking the piss. These are just
games that we play to keep us amused.

In Circus Town, real names are for the past and the
unfairly accused

and there's no reply from the grave whatever name is
used.

Fat Frank takes out another tin can and passes it to
Cheddar.

Cheddar is a loner, he's nobody's wing man, he's as
free as the wind, yet he's come to cherish his
place on the bench.

He takes the tin can and holds it close in an unsteady
clench,

he has a touch of the shakes and feels a bit worse for
wear,

but Cheddar still has what it takes to live without care,

he's a ducker and diver, he's a natural born survivor.

And he has earned his name because of all the

cheese that he stole

it was easy to steal and Cheddar couldn't always rely
    on the dole

because he lived off the grid, didn't join in the race,

he was the invisible kid always hiding his face,

he was smoke, he was mist, he was living the dream,

and would choke on his own fist before he'd let you
    hear a scream.

To him, silence was king, he believed in the still of
    night.

He'd seen too much violence, lost too many friends to
    the fight.

Cheddar was always alert, ready to move, ready to fly,

as he clenched his tin can watching the world passing
    by.

Fat Frank bends down and gives the last tin can to
    Tesco Sue.

She looks to be in her late forties but is only thirty two.

They called her Tesco Sue because she gave special
    offers, like two-for-one.

She thought doing two together would save time,
    would only last half as long

and it didn't take much for her to forget what had been
    inside her,

all it took was a couple of litres of extra strong cider.

She had once been television pretty, back in the day,

until a drunk driver had taken her family away.

And yes, she saw the irony in becoming a drunk
      herself,

but managed to hold back the laughter each time she
      took a bottle off the shelf

but that's what it took for her to find a little peace,

some stole moments while others stole cheese

and it was okay. Because Fat Frank and Cheddar
      were family now.

And she would have told them she loved them – if she
      hadn't forgotten how.

These three bench dwellers are just watching as the
      world passes by,

and just like the rest of us, they live, they die.

But these keen observers are not what you may think,

they're not just dodgers and skivers lost to the drink,

and they're not tabled in the neatness of government
      statistics,

because you can't count the incompleteness of
      ethereal mystics,

these great philosophers, these owls of the road
where they've paid the price of expectations, and
    nothing is owed.
So don't hurry past, it won't hurt you if you look them
    in the eye,
and you don't need to explain a donation, they already
    know what you're trying to buy,
they do not want your sympathy but they will accept
    your coin,
their club is members only, they know you're not
    subscribing to join,
and they have all of life's answers, but how can they
    share them with you, when you won't look them
    in the eye?
They are just sat watching as the world and his dog
    are passing by

The Wolf Man has concluded his business with the
    Circus Town royalty.
He had given them coin but it's reputation that buys
    Circus Town loyalty,
and now the intrepid travellers head back to their slice
    of heaven, me, the Wolf Man, and

Frankenstein's Bride.
I reach my door. The Wolf Man passes me my
    luggage and I go inside.
This is Circus Town, this is my town.
I am Circus Town.

I am home .
I want a takeaway.
But I've sold my phone.
Scooby fuckin' Doo.

I wake in the blades of night to a sun exploding dark.
I feel my skin spark and it's blood corroding.
And I itch and itch and itch, because I'm just a glitch in
    natural selection I'm a colour blind dyslexic
    stuck on auto-correction, I'm Scooby Scooby
    Doo stuck on Shaggy's erection coo coo ca
    fuckin choo and her whose name I cannot say is
    a fat Cinderella in a thin person's shoe and I tell
    her a different version than the one I tell you
    because she's Helen Keller and she's found the

last clue and I'm boiling up I'm boiling up I'm
boiling up and I can see the Gingerbread Man.
The Wolf Man came around today.
He took my television
and left a bruise.

The Frankstein's Bride tried to kiss me today.
I shouted into her black eye face and pushed her
away.
I doubted very much that we should be adding to the
human race.
Her tongue lashed back and her broken wings
unfurled,
but I wouldn't go along with risking bringing another
Circus Town freak into the world.
She started crying, sour tears on soured cheek, and I
laughed and I laughed at her gibbering beak and
brown wings.
There was no room in my head for other things, and
Circus Town has enough sideshows, bearded
ladies and abortionists, homemade chemists
and contortionists, so roll up roll up see

someone else's show buy some candy floss and
the Wolf Man's snow, Circus Town, Circus Town
open every day of the year enjoy the freak show
and the fun of the fair.
There's enough side shows and slide shows inside my
head inside my head inside my head so I tell
Frankenstein's Bride to fuck off and I go to bed.
I go to bed.

Last night, her whose name I cannot say came.
She was limping.

I chased the postman today.

No reason.
I just thought it would be funny.

We are not the main course.

We are the leftovers.

The space debris.

Result of collision and percussion.

The shrapnel.

And how the fern did laugh at the tumbling fools.

How they pointed at swimmers and belly crawlers,

the unsatisfied

wood and sand and impatient rock.

Grip and grunt and alliances,

the dawnbreakers.

Chop and carve and fence and dig

and how the fern did sigh at the grazing blind.

How they ignored gatherers and throwers.

The Gods.

Colours painting themselves

around rainbow specks

through a chameleon eye.

The conquerors.

The rock dripped and in an eon's pause.

Swimmers and belly crawlers stood taller in the sun.

Refurbishing and defining.

The pushers.

Wood turned to paper to words.

To backs turned.

Test tube imitations and two-headed sheep.
Summer fruit on Winter's day,
but shhh! Don't tell the rhubarb,
the illusionists,
the space debris that we are .
Backstabbers, the gatherers of silver,
picnickers and day-trippers.
Daisy chain murderers,
and another petal falls,
and how the fern did laugh,
and how the fern did cry.

Coo coo ca fuckin' choo.

I've been to the Wolf Man's.
He's out.

I've been to the Wolf Man's.
He's out.

I've been to the Wolf man's.
He's out.
I kiss Frankenstein's Bride.

Scooby Doo got work to do.

Last night, her whose name I cannot say came.
She has a million words and plenty to say.
She was a little perturbed my head wasn't empty.
For last night I was holding a convention of those I
      cannot bury, and those I shouldn't mention, my
      sexual partners, my lovers, the nearly
      acceptable and the nearly new mothers, my
      rumbles and tumbles and Circus Town fumbles,
      the midnight voices and second choices and
      bareback rides with clumsy fingers, the sour lip
      smack of cunnilingus and on they came, the
      right and the wrong and I tell her how I lost my
      virginity to the Avon lady, ding fuckin' dong, and
      her whose name I cannot say found there wasn't
enough of me to stay.

But she wins hands down, she's the blood that runs
through Circus Town, it scars with its
unwashable stain.
In a flash of night, all the ghosts are gone, except one,
one memory still remains. Susan Jenkins.
Susan Jenkins was in class three.
She'd show you her pants for 50p,
and what was inside for double the free, and she only
had one eye.
When she was twelve she grew big breasts,
we drew pictures of them on our desks,
she got bullied by the girls who had flat chests, and
she only had one eye.
At age fourteen I took Susan Jenkins on a date,
she brought along her fat best mate,
but I copped a feel outside her gate, and she only had
one eye.
We went on our own to watch Rambo 3,
she put my hand on her bare knee,
And she tossed me off in row 43, and she only had
one eye.
She agreed to go out with me again,
we said we would meet down Lover's Lane,
but she had left me waiting in the rain, and she only

had one eye.

She ignored me at school the very next day,

and I knew there was nothing that I could say,

for where she was going was a world away, and she

only had one eye.

When she was fifteen she left the school,

and left me feeling like a love-struck fool,

but I pretended I was Fonzie cool, and she only had

one eye.

I saw Susan Jenkins when she was sixteen,

she had the hardest looking boyfriend I'd ever seen,

he was covered in tattoos and was pit-bull mean, and

she only had one eye.

I saw her a year later in the street,

she had six inch pink heels on her feet,

she looked so tired but still as sweet, and she only

had one eye.

Someone told me that she had a kid,

and she'd have sex with you for fifty quid,

and I realised then how far she'd slid and she only

had one eye.

Susan Jenkins OD'ed on coke and ecstacy,

died alone in a bedsit aged twenty three,

but she had seen things I'd never see and she only

had one eye.

In the glaring darkness of a sweat stained night,
I give a silent toast to Circus Town royalty.
Coo coo ca fuckin' choo Susan Jenkins,
coo coo ca fuckin' choo.

I went to see Frankenstein's Bride today.
She was out.

I went to see Frankenstein's Bride today.
She was out.

I went to see Frankenstein's Bride today.
She was out.
The Wolf Man asked me in.
Scooby fuckin' doo.

Hey hey hey Mr Rent Man, what yer gonna do?

You want the rent but the money is spent,

coo coo ca fuckin' choo.

Hey hey hey, Scooby Scooby Doo,

you and me are going to live in the Circus Town zoo.

We will dance with the liar who lives in the moon,

and build a fire to put under our spoon.

I'm going to bed inside my head I'm going to bed.

I never cried when my dad was dead.

I never cried when my dad was dead.

Just over the scar unwithered red,

and the millions of words I never said,

beneath the grey of an unnecessary day,

I'm just an atom on the wind that's blowing me away,

that's blowing me away that's blowing me away,

that's

blowing

me

away like a cheap Circus Town whore

that's

blowing

me

away through a party straw.

Buffeting me through the Circus Town air, but I know
    how to tough it out now I'm royalty in the Wolf
    Man's lair where I know how to bluff it to get my
    fair share so blow me away. I just don't care
    inside my head I just don't care inside my head.

The postman punched me in the face today.
Return to sender, love me tender.
The king is dead all hail the pretender.
Hail

The light bulb has blown.
All the light bulbs must have blown.
No.
No no no no no no.
It's a conspiracy.
Someone not someone the government someone has
    stolen my electricity and put holes in my shoes
    and hidden my Weetabix and taken my Scooby
    Scooby Doos and… and.. and…
They've put a spider in my bath.
The bastards.

A spider, a spider, I think it's electronic.

Sonic.

It's got a camera on it.

It's reporting back it's reporting back and I can't kill it I
    can't kill it it's got a thousand baby cameramen
    living in it that will come bursting out of its gut
    and I can see them I can see them even though
    I've got my eyes shut waiting to bore into my
    eyes and tunnel up my butt to get inside me
    inside me inside my head and tell the men in
    suits I never cried for the really dead and just for
    the scar unwithered red and will take me away
    from the Circus Town beat and bring me her
    whose name I cannot say so I can fall at her feet
    and touch the flesh and bones of a living ghost
    while the Wolf Man eats dead sparrows on
    Scooby Scooby Doo toast... The bastards.

The Wolf Man smiled at me today.

Frankenstein's Bride did not.

I wake up, which is funny.

I didn't know I was asleep.

The spider has gone,

no it hasn't,

I'm inside the spider,

no I'm not.

Circus Town is the spider.

Today I know it was just a fucking spider.

But it can't be today because yesterday was today,

     and tomorrow?

Tomorrow is the moon.

My furniture is in the garden

my frying pan's in a box.

Excuse me, beg your pardon,

but have you seen my socks?

Coo coo ca fuckin' choo

I knock knock knock on the Wolf Man's door

and am welcomed in by the Wolf Man's paw

and as my eyes adjust to the Wolf Man's lair

I see a freak who's escaped from the Circus Town
    fair.
Who's he? Why is he stroking Scooby Scooby Doo's
    hair,
and why does he stare, and… and… and…
and he plunged
and he plunged and he plunged and he plunged
    headfirst into black pools of unbled thirst and
    into the empty arms of angels lost and cursed.
He took long gulps of air reserved for kings and fools
    and looked upon the broken wings and heard
    words spoken too loudly for little things.
And he surfaced amongst the crowd of monsters slain
    and proudly danced in the mist of a psychedelic
    rain kissing the bending arc of a dead rainbow's
    strain.
He reached out to these descending angels who had
    travelled forth to make corpse angels in the
    wave-thrown sands of itching time and they
    welcomed him to their joyous band.
And he travelled.
And he travelled and he travelled and he travelled far,
    hitching his wagon to their extinguished star as
    he wished and wished and wished for a star of

his own to follow in the tangerine sky of orange
dark.

He led the way, tasting the swallow of a bleeding
spark that bled from the receding sky above the
joyous band of the fallen and the dead.

And he wished.

And he wished and he wished and he wished and he
wished away all the wishes he never had as he
knelt beside a turquoise tree and fished for stars
inside a dried up well so he could speak a
million words that had nothing to say to the
ghosts he knew so well and ghosts he'd never
met.

He felt the punchlines to jokes he'd never get and saw
the lines he'd not yet crossed and wished and
wished he could reach into the heaven's maw
and find new worlds for the joyous band of the
fallen and the dead to explore.

And on.

And on and on and on and on he travelled with this
joyous band through silvered plasma and
unwithered scars, through the miasma of
nebulae until he found a station in the
stratosphere between drear ghouls and vile

ghosts and saw the revelations of kings and
fools marked on the mileposts that led the way
to destinations and journey's end.

He saw his expectations bend as he unravelled his
own constraints and he reached for the loose
threads of those entombed saints who had
come before, Saints who had been consumed
by fire and broken on the wheel and who had
now awoken to the surreal choir of the joyous
band that travelled deeper and deeper and
deeper and higher and higher until they could
feel the ground that was fifty million feet away.

And he waved his hand through the multi-coloured
waves of sound at the ants below who were
making ant corpses in the sand.

And he dived.

And he dived and he dived and he dived higher and
higher and higher until he found a treasure trove
of earth and fire where he danced on the
boulders that had grown on the shifting ground
of weeping bones.

He felt the drifting cries below his lifting feet that
kicked sleeping stones which stirred the rebirth
of stars and planets and spirals and galaxies

and universes that spurred on his travelling
joyous band.

He heard the corpse angels' forgotten words as they
twirled and swirled and curled around him as he
unfurled his broken wings and flew into the
tourmalines and opalines and melting greens,
adding his own voice to the inbetween,
harmonising with the travelling band's fanfare for
the coming of the kings and queens of ants.

And he danced.

And he danced and he danced and he danced on
these well-trodden paths of ants and those other
saints that had chanced the odds on the holy
trails of smaller gods.

He heard the echoes of their ecstatic wails and silent
screams as he danced and danced and danced
on galactic beams and golden gates that led the
way to violent dreams where he would taste the
colours of the dead that pulsate and purr and fall
before his eyes like a dragon's scales that
pierce the ants who quail beneath the parting of
vermilion seas.

He reverberates in the wreath of smoke that a million
corpse angels descend to breathe and dances

like Fred Astaire as his top hat falls and falls fifty
million feet into the air.
And he reached.
And he reached and he reached and he reached and
he grasped for the touch of ants as the colours
bleached from a bruising sky.
He clasped his hands in sorrow to find that these
colours that leeched to dust had only been his to
borrow and he cried and he cried at all the rust
and the coming grey shadows of brighter days
that had died amongst the corpse angels must,
their broken wings embracing smaller gods and
that had rocked the ants awake.
He cocked an expectant ear, hoping to hear the fallen
and the dead,
but they had ceased to dance, they would no longer
feast on the last chance that he'd supplied. They
had broken up the travelling joyous band of
fallen angels and the ants who had made
corpses in the sand.
He waited,
and waited and waited and waited and nothing more.
And nothing more.
He had seen the universe, and wanted to find others

to explore.

He watched.

He watched and watched and watched as the sky
dissipated, watched the looming dark as
tangerine fades and nothing more,
no more the luminescent shades of neon blues and
bleeding reds,
no crescent blades of pulsating suns, no effervescent
stars with their finishing bursts of unnamed
hues,
and nothing more,
just black pools of unbled thirst.

And he begged.

And he begged and he begged and he begged on
broken knees before the fading outlines of
golden gates and the diminishing echoes of the
screams of the fallen and the lost from their
unfaithful dreams that drowned out the beams of
the tired stars,
and nothing more.

And nothing more
… just a pulling sensation
Just a pulling sensation forcing him through the black
pool's crust, culling his senses one by one, until

he fears that all will be gone.

He hears the cold before he feels it.

A last sensation before the crushing black steals it, to
replace it with a rushing, gushing pain, the
deceleration pushing and pushing again and
again and again he feels in every crack and
every pore,

and nothing more.

Each sense is becoming but one sense.

It offers no counter-attack or defence because he
knows he cannot catch the tail of this rabid dog
that has gripped him in its immense and
salivating jaw, for it has stripped him and ripped
him from the broken wings of the fallen and the
dead,

and nothing more.

He cries.

And he cries and he cries and he cries and he cries
for those good old days of tangerine skies where
he had led the way for the joyous band that
travelled high above the ants as the fallen
angels had unravelled the shrouds of those
other saints and had danced and danced and
danced without the restraints of love and hope

and who had chanced the holy trails of ghouls
and ghosts, emboldened fools and the golden
gates of golden hosts all shining brightly in the
fresh-faced boasts of kaleidoscopes and
psychedelic paints.

He cries for these saints and their mileposts.

And he laughs.

And he cries for those well-trodden paths and nothing
more.

The laughter sounds like somebody elses. It can't be
his, for he never got the jokes that did the
rounds, it was only after the laughs had died
was he told their meaning.

So he knows it is not laughter.

He knows it is not laughter.

He knows he is crying.

And he cried.

And he cries and he cries and he cries in pain and
fear,

in fear of never again dancing like Fred Astaire,
dropping his top hat fifty million feet into the air.

He cries for punchlines and smaller gods.

He cries for the fallen with their broken wings who
made corpse angels in the sand.

And I cry.

And I cry and I cry and I cry and I cry as the Wolf Man
    puts another needle in my hand.

Eeny meeny, Scooby Doo

I'm going to bed I'm going to bed to forget all the
    things I never said inside my head inside my
    head are the ghosts of those who are undead
    and those still waiting for me to say goodbye
    and kiss the dead inside my bed inside my bed
    but this is not my bed this is not my bed this bed
    is yours this bed's not mine someone's awoken
    me and the bed's not mine and someone has
    broken Frankenstein's Bride and opened the
    Wolf Man so I can see inside I can see inside
    there's a smile in his stomach and the smile is
    wide and leaking on the ground but I don't care
    coz I'm the freaking king of Circus Town inside
    my head inside my head I didn't kiss my dad
    when he was dead I didn't kiss my dad when he

was dead I didn't...
What's that? What's that?
It's not the Wolf Man blowing down the door,
I don't think we're talking anymore.
Who is it? Who is it with their urgent paw?
I know I know it's the spider in the bath,
it saw it saw the spider saw.
It's reported back it's reported back,
run Scooby Doo run run Scooby Doo,
catch the coo coo ca fuckin' choo
I'm the new king of Circus Town, I'm fucking royalty,
my kingdom is built on treachery and loyalty,
I have silver in my hand and gold in my head
I'm going to travel with the joyous band to where the
　　　　black pools bled
Who are you? Who are you? Who are you?
You're not Scooby Scooby Doo.

Have you come to take me home?

They have moved me.

Given me pills to improve me, soothe me.

And though they disapprove of me, they have tried to
learn the truth of me.

Her whose name I cannot say has stayed with me all
these years.

I kept her hidden from the probers in their comfy
chairs.

She's my ghost, not theirs,

I gave them other stuff to keep them satisfied,
convincing them I was giving enough of my
inside.

But I didn't give them her

I am back in Circus Town.

Same names but different faces,

playing the same games, the hidden aces,

Circus Town still beats with its greasy thrum.

Easy go and easy come.

Better for others and worse for some,

we share our history, but not our future, but it still runs
in my veins.

Because once you've travelled the worlds beyond,

Circus Town is all that remains,
Circus Town is all.

I have a new neighbour now.
She is an old woman, tired like me.
Unlike me, she has pictures on her wall.
She has family: people who will kiss her corpse
… There it is…
I was waiting… tock.
I'm going to bed.

Where are you Scooby Scooby Doo?
We'll miss the train that goes coo coo ca choo.
I never cried for my dead dad
Boo hoo ca fuckin' boo.

The tick

The tock

Oh Daddy Daddy, won't you sit me on your knees,

pick a book and read to me please,

we will sail our ship on the seven seas

and swing with Mowgli through the trees .

But you're dead, aren't you Dad?

And I gave you to them,

because I couldn't give them her.

She fills the gap between the tick and the tock,

so I gave them you.

I loved a dead German film star once.

I loved you once too, but I didn't know why.

I lay in my bed and listen to Circus Town, awake to a
    mother's cry.

It doesn't break my heart, just my will.

I still see the ghosts that I can't kill.

Especially those who are not yet dead.

Inside my head inside my head.

I welcome her whose name I cannot say inside my
    head.

I stare at the hole in the rug.

It resembles the shape of a country,

though I don't know which one.

A world at my feet and a world outside my door,

I couldn't decide which one scared me more,

which one had lied the most.

My bed creaks in protest as I change position,

rusted bones and broken frames.

I watch the tock… and wait for the tick,

I count thick seconds, and feel the hours.

It will be dark soon

and I will walk to the park.

This day will not be the same.

Because every day is the same.

My head hurt, it was full of the empty.

Oh they had given me pills, pills a plenty,

blue ones, yellow ones, red and white ones

square ones. Round and oval ones.

They sat in boxes with the days written on them,

salvation by calendar,

a damnation by diary, I thought sourly.

A multi-coloured reminder of what I fought hourly.

And lost.

A tray of designer happiness, normality at any cost,

squares and ovals, circles of hilarity,

drugs to cope. Cope with what though?

The world in my rug? The world outside my door?

The world and its dog with its salivating jaw?

Who can ever cope with that?

It will be dark soon.

I will stare Circus Town in the face, and I will walk to
     the park.

My head hurts, it is full of the empty.

But not pills, oh no.

No pills today.

No pills a-plenty for Christopher Becker.

The trays were still full of happy days,

and the unknown world in the rug was trying to draw
          me in and the world outside my door was
          closing in and the world and his dog were crying
          in sin and despair that Christopher Becker
          wasn't there.

I heard my name.

Christopher Becker Christopher Becker Christopher
          Becker

and realise I am shouting it out aloud,

hating the sound of it,

hating the feel of it on my tongue.

Christopher Becker Christopher Becker,

wrong wrong wrong.

A name that doesn't fit,

I recount seconds,

feel the hours that amount to nothing,

except the tick, the tock.

My head was full of the empty and I am tired,

but I am not going to bed.

I want to be awake when it's time to sleep,

because it will be dark soon

and I will walk through the streets of Circus Town to
    the park,

where Christopher Becker will claim his moon.

ABOUT THE AUTHOR

This is Robbies 3rd book. He is known for his comedy poetry but this is the sort of work that he wants to write, where the humour is where you find it and not given to you.

Robbie started his writing on the back of an envelope at Lincoln Creative Writers, adamant that it wasn't for him. Four years later, having not missed a monthly meeting he is working on book number four.

Printed in Great Britain
by Amazon